One Day in Japan with

HOKUSAI

Prestel

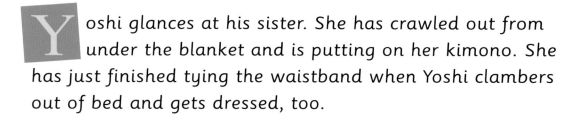

Kiku and Yoshi are off to visit their grandfather today. They are very excited and wake up much earlier than usual. From the clatter of pans coming from the kitchen they can tell that their mother is preparing breakfast and the smell of boiled rice, fish and vegetables fills the house. Yoshi's tummy starts rumbling—they don't normally have such a big breakfast, he thinks. The tasty treats are in fact for the children to take with them for their grandfather.

Yoshi glances at his sister. She has crawled out from under the blanket and is putting on her kimono. She has just finished tying the waistband when Yoshi clambers out of bed and gets dressed, too.

This morning they only need to wash their hands and faces as they went to the bath-house yesterday in the evening so as to be squeaky-clean for their visit to their grandfather.

菱原業孝

君か為め
をしから
命さへ
ながくも
かな

花ゝゝ卍

During breakfast Kiku and Yoshi's mother tells them quite clearly that they are not to rush around too much at their grandfather's. He can sometimes be a bit moody and works the whole day from dawn to dusk. Although he is now over eighty, he still draws and paints a great deal. Kiku and Yoshi are terribly proud of their grandfather. His name is Hokusai and he is a very famous master of the woodblock print and a painter. Many people in the city know his name.

When they are ready, their mother gives them a basket of food to take with them. They don't have far to go and they have been there many times before with their mother. But today they are being allowed to go on their own for the first time.

E ven though it is still early in the morning, the streets are packed with people. There are masses of boats out on the River Sumida which flows through the city. We are in Edo, which is now called Tokyo. It is a huge city, full of people selling all sorts of things.

Kiku and Yoshi have to go over several bridges on their way. Most of the bridges in Japan are made of wood and are humpbacked, rising steeply in the middle.

On one of the bridges there is a beautiful woman in a red kimono, tied together with a blue waistband. She has a number of pins in her hair which looks very pretty. She doesn't seem to be bothered by the crowds around about. Instead she is deep in thought and gazes into the distance. On the horizon, the holy mountain Fuji can be seen, all ablaze in the red of the rising sun.

On seeing this, Yoshi has to think of the many woodblock prints that his grandfather has done of Mount Fuji. The picture of the volcano bathed in red is very famous.

A ll of a sudden, someone bumps into Yoshi from behind. He turns around in surprise. A man has pushed him out of the way so that three young men, who are rolling barrels along in front of them, can get past.

I t must be very tiring as the barrels are heavy and the road is rather bumpy. Yoshi turns to his sister but Kiku has disappeared. He is worried and runs across to the other side of the river where there are fewer people, but he cannot see Kiku anywhere. Not quite sure which way to go, he runs along the bank to where there is a small temple. Two men are sitting at the entrance, facing inwards.

A lady and a gentleman are taking a stroll past the temple. But Yoshi is too shy to ask them if they have seen his sister. Without knowing what he should do he turns round and round in circles. Suddenly he sees his sister standing next to a fence, peeking into the garden beyond. He runs up to her and is just about to tell her off when he notices that she must have followed the beautiful lady from the bridge who is just going into the house.

"Come on! We have to get to grand-dad's soon. If you keep on running off like that, we'll never get there!" With a deep sigh Kiku lets Yoshi tug her away by the hand. "Older brothers can be a big bore sometimes," she thinks. At the next street corner, they come across a mass of people gathered around a large gateway. Full of curiosity, Kiku and Yoshi push their way through the crowd. In front of them, on a small hill in the middle of a large park, they can see that a stage has been built. Two women holding brightly colored fans in their hands are performing a dance. Their hair is so long that it almost touches the ground. They are accompanied by six musicians, who are sitting behind them on the stage. Kiku and Yoshi watch them with their eyes open wide—they have never seen a dance like this before.

Then, all of a sudden, one of the noblemen in the garden notices the unwelcome guests peeking through the gateway. He jumps up and orders a servant to close the gates properly. "What a shame," think the children.

But when they look across the road they see their Aunt Oei on the other side. She has just been collecting water from the well and is carrying a wooden bucket in one hand. The children run over to her and give her a big, warm hug. Aunt Oei lives with the children's grandfather and so Kiku and Yoshi go back to the house with her.

The two children are very excited about seeing their grandfather. They rush into the house, calling his name. Hokusai is sitting in his studio, completely lost in his work. Every now and then he dips a brush into a pot of ink and confidently draws a line on a sheet of paper. Kiku and Yoshi sneak up behind him. They can't make out what Hokusai is painting since it looks very different from anything else that they have ever seen their grandfather do before. Hesitantly, they peer a little closer. "I know what it is!" Yoshi exclaims. "It's a map."

Hokusai drops the brush in surprise! He was so caught up with his work that he hadn't even noticed the children! He is happy to see the two of them and says: "I thought that you were never going to get here! Come and sit over here with me." He pushes some sheets of paper to one side, and Kiku and Yoshi sit down.

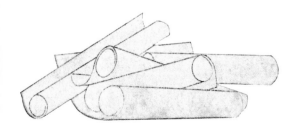

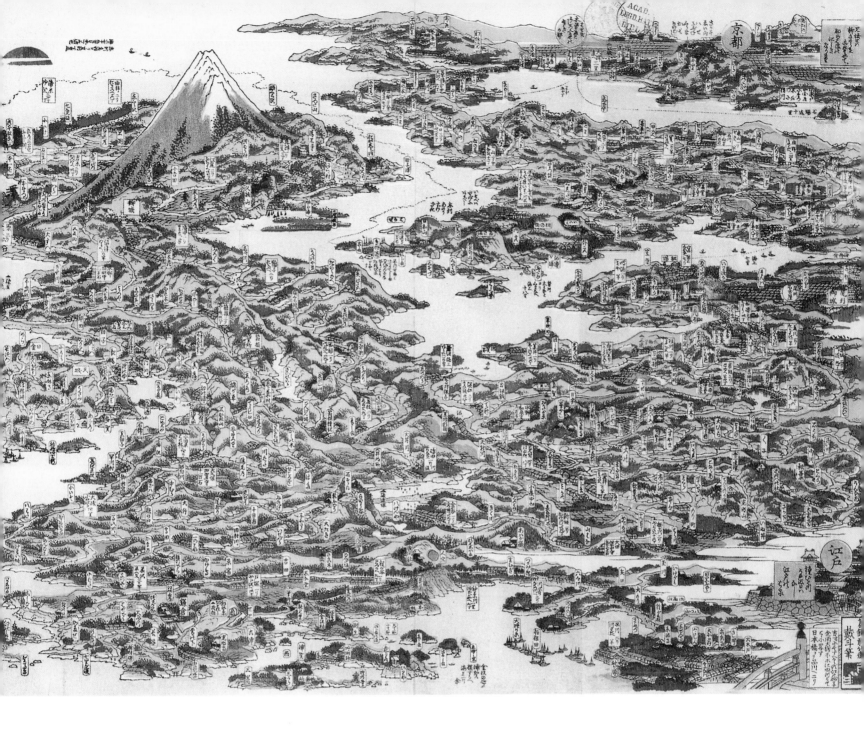

H e shows the two children the map, which clearly marks the famous Tokaido Road, linking the towns of Edo and Kyoto. All over the map Hokusai has added the names of the best-known places in little boxes.

A little later, Aunt Oei calls out that lunch is ready. She has unpacked the basket of food that the children brought with them and prepared everything for the others. Kiku and Yoshi now realize how hungry they are. Before starting, they wash their hands in a small tub of water. During the meal, the adults hardly talk at all—but you can tell from the slurping and chomping how much they like their food!

Yoshi looks out of the window. On the other side of the road there is a big sawmill. Beyond it is a workshop owned by a man called Mr. Tsutaya. He is a publisher who prints a lot of Hokusai's pictures and sells them. Yoshi feels rather uncomfortable whenever he thinks of Mr. Tsutaya.

H e once visited the publisher with his grandfather who was there to tell the woodcutters what they had to do. Yoshi was bored. He would have preferred to have seen how prints are made from the woodblocks. But the printers didn't have any time for him. They were in the middle of printing a picture with twelve different colors. They had to be very careful that the sheets were in the right position on the woodblocks for each of the different colors to be printed. Yoshi wanted to get a better view and clambered up to the top of a high stack of boxes. He lent over the edge a little too far and everything started to wobble and then came tumbling down. There were boxes all over workshop! Mr. Tsutaya was not very happy at all!

Yoshi can see Mount Fuji from his grandfather's house. He has always wanted to go there—and it's not real. that far away either. You can actually get there and back in a day, but Yoshi has never been out of the city. Secretly he dreams of being a warrior and of exploring the big, wide world. He imagines having his own horse and servants, who would travel with him. And of course he would have lots of adventures and become a great hero.

Y oshi's biggest hero is called Kintaro, who as a young boy lived with his mother in the mountains where he learned to tame wild animals. One day Prince Minamoto no Yorimitsu came across the young boy and invited him back to his palace. He gave him the best teachers in the country and Kintaro grew up to become a famous general.

K intaro could also fight spirits and demons. In one old tale all he had to do was scatter some beans in the path of the demons and that was enough to scare them off!

While Yoshi was dreaming away, Kiku was telling Aunt Oei about their mother. A few weeks earlier she had made a pilgrimage to Enoshima. A pilgrimage is a journey which people make to a shrine or other sacred place.

Enoshima, a small peninsula jutting out into the sea, is the home of the Japanese goddess of fortune, Benten. Inside a cave there is a statue of the goddess. It is only ever shown to the public every few years and there is a big festival each time.

A few days later, Kiku went with her mother to the famous temple of Asakusa where there was a huge crowd of people who all wanted to pray in front of the big hall in the temple. Kiku found it all very exciting, especially the traveling sales people and the monks who sold charms to the visitors.

There were also scribes at the temple who write letters for people who cannot write and then they read them out aloud. Kiku didn't want to have to go back home again—there were simply so many interesting things to see!

Hokusai is listening carefully to his little granddaughter. He then sweeps his hand through his unruly hair and begins to tell a story: "When I was young, I also liked to travel around. I journeyed along the Tokaido Road as far as Kyoto and Osaka." The children love it when their grandfather tells them stories about his trips. In his studio he keeps a box of pictures he made on these journeys. He drew pictures of the posting stations along the route, showing the famous landmarks of each place.

"My journey was not easy in those days. There were not many horses or carriages. I had to carry my own luggage on my back. And the route was quite dangerous, too. I once had to cross a wide river, but there were no boats. So I went to the next crossing point where bearers were waiting. They used to carry the travelers and their baggage across the river. The river was flowing very fast that day and it was so deep that the water reached right up to the bearer's chin. He had to turn back and I had to wait several days until I could eventually cross the river."

"Many of the people who traveled in those days were tradespeople," the grandfather continues. "They used to sell their goods in the larger towns and cities. These were times of peace; there were no wars or uprisings against the shogun—the military governor who ruled Japan—so the merchants used to earn a lot of money. There were also lots of pilgrims out and about, who were visiting the different temples, shrines, and holy waterfalls. But some people traveled simply for pleasure, visiting famous places and going to festivals in different towns, or they just enjoyed being out in the beautiful countryside. When the cherry trees blossom in the spring, many people go to Yoshino to marvel at the oceans of blossom that make the countryside look as if it is covered in snow."

Most of all, Hokusai likes telling stories about the wind and everything that it can do. "Once the wind was so strong that everyone had to hold onto their hats very tightly. There was a young lady who was walking along in front of me when suddenly her kimono was caught by the wind! She was so surprised that she let go of the pile of paper she was carrying—it was so funny to see all the sheets dancing around up in the air!"

He also has some stories to tell about the sea. "When there is a storm at sea, the waves are sometimes swept into mountain-like peaks with deep hollows between them. The sea may look very exciting but it is also very dangerous. When fishermen are caught in a storm out at sea, they can't always get back to land for some time. Once, when I was out in a boat myself, it was tossed about so much that I was very seasick and went all green in the face!"

Kiku and Yoshi are fascinated by their grandfather's stories.

"Time's getting on," Aunt Oei says all of a sudden. "You should be heading off home now before it gets dark." Hokusai quickly writes a note to the children's mother to thank her for the excellent food. Then he slips a couple of his drawings into the basket as presents for the children.

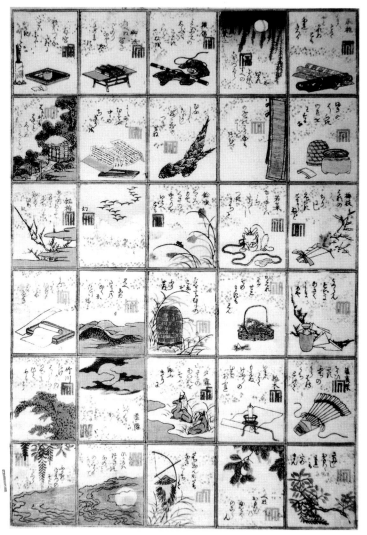

One of them is a card game that he has made especially for Kiku and Yoshi. But before they can start to play with it they will have to cut out the different squares. The children would like to try it out straight away.

Aunt Oei gives both of them small cakes of rice and packs them off. Kiku and Yoshi rush back without stopping on the way. By the time they get home, they are tired but happy after this long day.

Katsushika Hokusai, Japan's most famous artist, was born in 1760 in Edo, present-day Tokyo. As a young boy he seems to have been adopted into the Nakajima family. After training as a woodblock-cutter he was taken on by the artist Katsukawa Shunsho as a print designer, probably at the age of nineteen. Hokusai was interested in many different artistic styles which led to difficulties with Katsukawa and he eventually had to leave the workshop.

As well as Chinese painting, Hokusai studied the artistic styles of the West. He used different artist's names for the new styles he tried out, or for certain individual works. In 1796, he first adopted the name Hokusai. He often illustrated popular novels by some of his author friends, such as Kyokutei Bakin and Ryutei Tanehiko.

From 1820 onwards, Hokusai suffered personal and financial problems, but also created some of his best-known works such as *The Thirty-Six Views of Mount Fuji*. After her divorce, Oei, one of his daughters, returned to live with Hokusai. The artist moved house frequently and, because he received very little pay, he was always in debt. Another strike of ill-fortune was a fire in his home in 1839, in which all the works of art he had assembled since childhood were destroyed.

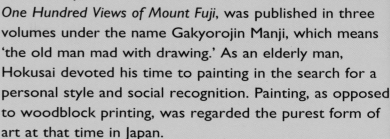

At this time he was making virtually no individual prints, working only on book illustrations. His masterpiece of book illustration, *One Hundred Views of Mount Fuji*, was published in three volumes under the name Gakyorojin Manji, which means 'the old man mad with drawing.' As an elderly man, Hokusai devoted his time to painting in the search for a personal style and social recognition. Painting, as opposed to woodblock printing, was regarded the purest form of art at that time in Japan.

Hokusai died on 10th May 1849, convinced that, had he had a little more time, he could have become a truly great artist.

GLOSSARY

ASAKUSA: a district of Tokyo.

BENTEN or BENZAITEN: the only goddess among the Seven Deities of Good Fortune.

EDO: present-day Tokyo, the capital city of Japan, seat of the military government headed by the shogun. The Edo period lasted from 1603 until 1867.

ENOSHIMA: peninsula near Tokyo, where the goddess Benten is worshipped.

INK: here also 'tusche,' made of soot, glue from bones and ethereal oil, mixed together with water and used for writing or painting, or as a wash.

KIMONO: an ankle-length garment with wide sleeves worn in Japan and tied with a wide waistband or sash.

KYOTO (or Kioto): former capital city and seat of the imperial family.

SHRINE: here, wooden structures of differing sizes which are the 'homes' of the gods worshipped in Shintoism, the religion native to Japan.

TEMPLE: a building for worshipping a god or gods, here, in Buddhism, a religion introduced into Japan by way of China in the 6th century AD.

TOKAIDO ROAD: a major inland route from Edo to Kyoto with a number of posting stations along the way.

WOODBLOCK PRINT (*okiyo-e*): a type of woodcut printed from separate wooden blocks, each carrying a separate color and fitted together to make the complete design, with one color sometimes overlapping another. The motif is drawn by the artist and positioned on a piece of wood. The blockcutter carves the wood through the paper removing those areas not to be printed. The raised parts are inked and a printout made. The artist then decides which areas are to be colored and the cutter makes separate woodblocks for each color. Between 150 and 200 prints can be made from each block. The finished prints are then marketed by a publisher.